PAUL MACKAY, born 1946 in Hong Kong, studied economics in the Netherlands and business administration in France. After working in international finance, he met and studied Anthroposophy in England and Germany between 1974 and 1977. From 1977 until 2012 he was active in anthroposophical banking, as co-founder and Executive Director of Triodos Bank in the Netherlands, and then Executive Director of GLS Bank in Germany, and later Chairman of its supervisory Board. As of March 2012 he is President of the Board of Directors of Weleda AG in Switzerland. In 1996 Paul Mackay joined the Executive Council of the General Anthroposophical Society at the Goetheanum, Switzerland. In 2000 he additionally became leader of the Section for Social Sciences of the School of Spiritual Science.

THE ANTHROPOSOPHICAL SOCIETY AS A MICHAEL COMMUNITY

On the Word 'We' in the Foundation Stone Meditation

Paul Mackay

TEMPLE LODGE

Translated by Douglas Miller

Temple Lodge Publishing
Hillside House, The Square
Forest Row, RH18 5ES

www.templelodge.com

Published by Temple Lodge 2013

© Verlag am Goetheanum 2002
This translation © Temple Lodge Publishing 2013

Paul Mackay asserts his moral right to be identified as the author of this work

All rights reserved. No part of this publication may be reproduced, stored in a retrieval system, or transmitted, in any form or by any means, electronic, mechanical, photocopying or otherwise, without the prior permission of the publishers

The blackboard drawings by Rudolf Steiner are reproduced by kind permission of the Rudolf Steiner Nachlassverwaltung, Dornach. They derive from GA 260/1-10

A catalogue record for this book is available from the British Library

ISBN 978 1 906999 54 4

Cover by Andrew Morgan Design
Typeset by DP Photosetting, Neath, West Glamorgan
Printed and bound by Berforts Ltd., Herts.

Contents

Preface	1
Part One	3
Individuation and the Social Need of our Time	3
The Rhythms of the Foundation Stone and the Members of the Human Constitution	6
'We' As an Expression of Spirit Self Quality	15
Part Two	17
Rules and Exceptions in Karmic Relationships	17
Events in the Ninth Century	19
Events in the Fourth Century	21
The Mystery of Death and Evil	24
The Second Crucifixion and Resurrection	26
A Free-will Deed	27
Restoring the Truth of Karma	30
The Foundation Stone Meditation	34
Rudolf Steiner's Blackboard Drawings	38
Notes	45
Bibliography of books by Rudolf Steiner	49

Preface

Friends in the Czech Anthroposophical Society had asked me to give a lecture in Prague on 27 April 2001, on the theme of the Foundation Stone Meditation of the General Anthroposophical Society. I chose an approach to the rhythms of the Foundation Stone that I had never before encountered in the literature on the Foundation Stone.

I was led to this approach by a question about the word 'we' in the last part of the Foundation Stone: 'What we found from our hearts and direct from our heads with focused will.' How can this 'we' be understood? What characterizes this 'we?' In Part One, I would like to take this question as a point of departure in developing a specific approach to inner work with the rhythms of the Foundation Stone. This approach may lead to a sense for the quality of 'we'; it arose out of my experience of working with the seven rhythms of the Foundation Stone, for they seem to be an expression of the members of the human constitution—the 'we' in the fifth rhythm can then be understood as having the quality of Spirit Self.

Initially, the members present at the 1923–24 Christmas Foundation Meeting were addressed with this 'we'. But it also addresses all those who have since felt themselves connected with the impulse of the Christmas Foundation Meeting. In this context, I have tried in Part Two to view this 'we' from a karmic perspective. I have done so with reference to Rudolf Steiner's karma lectures which deal particularly with the karma of the Anthroposophical Society. What lies spiritually and cosmically at the foundation of a community like the Anthroposophical Society?

2 The Anthroposophical Society as a Michael Community

In wrestling with this question, I have come to the inner conviction that it is justified to speak of the Anthroposophical Society as a Michael community.

Paul Mackay
Dornach, 14 February 2002

Part One

Over the years, many friends have written about aspects of the Foundation Stone. For instance, F.W. Zeylmans van Emmichoven's little book *The Foundation Stone* appeared in 1956; among other things, he deals with the seven rhythms. He points to an inner activation of the I at the different levels of consciousness, and says that this can lead to a new spiritual constitution of the human body. Sergei Prokofieff's 1982 book *Rudolf Steiner and the Founding of the New Mysteries* describes how the rhythms are characteristic of the human path after death as well as the stages of a new Christian-Rosicrucian path of initiation. These two works provide sufficient reason to believe that the Foundation Stone rhythms indicated by Rudolf Steiner allow for different but complementary approaches for inner work with them.

Individuation and the Social Need of our Time

In his essay *Freedom and Society*,[1] Rudolf Steiner describes the 'basic sociological law' in the evolution of humanity:

> At the onset of culture, humanity strives to create social groups; that is when the interest of the individual is sacrificed to the interest of these groups. Further progress leads to freeing the individual from the interests of the group, and to a free development of individual needs and capacities.

> The basic sociological law is the law of individuation. This law comes to full expression in the cultural age of the

consciousness soul. Rudolf Steiner describes how human beings must now rely on themselves: just to maintain themselves in our time, human beings are led to a development of their antisocial drives.[2] Thus they are responsible for themselves. But then Rudolf Steiner adds that in an age requiring human beings to develop antisocial drives for their own sake it becomes all the more necessary to develop a conscious cultivation of the social element. The antisocial element occurs naturally; it comes with the development of the consciousness soul. The social element is a need; it requires cultivation. This social need is the indispensable counterweight in our time to the antisocial tendency in the development of humanity. Thus, according to Rudolf Steiner, the basic thrust of all social life today is in an interest that connects one human being with another. As contemporaries, we all find ourselves in this stage of development. In a 1923 lecture,[3] Rudolf Steiner complains of the way anthroposophists speak. He says:

> What's the use of telling people over and over that we're not a sect if we act like a sect? You see, something that needs to be well understood, especially by the members of the Anthroposophical Society, is what any society in our modern age requires. A society must not be a sect in any way. If the Anthroposophical Society is to stand on firm ground, the word 'we' can really never play a role in regard to opinion. Again and again, anthroposophists are heard saying to the rest of the world: 'We [the Society] think this or that. This or that is going on with us. We want this or that.' In earlier times, societies could present a face of conformity to the world. Now this is no longer possible. Within a contemporary society, each individual must really be a free human being. Only individuals have views, thoughts, and opinions. The

Society has no opinion. And that needs to be expressed in the language each individual uses about the Society. The 'we' really needs to disappear.

Here Rudolf Steiner speaks out clearly against group views or opinions in the Anthroposophical Society. Each person has his own opinion, one he has worked out for himself; he should feel responsible for what he represents as an individual. Thus it seems clear enough that the 'we' in the Foundation Stone does not refer to some group view held by 'anthroposophists'. What, then, is meant by 'we'?

In light of the fact that humanity is undergoing a process of individuation, and in view of the 1923 comment by Rudolf Steiner that every person in the Anthroposophical Society should really be a free human being, the word 'we' is lent a special quality in the Foundation Stone. It must be a 'we' that can take shape between free human beings on the principle of individuation.

Just after World War I, Rudolf Steiner asked the question: 'What is most deeply characteristic for our own time and for the development of the consciousness soul?' He answers this question by describing how the human being must become thoroughly and intensely familiar with the forces that would oppose the harmonizing of all humanity. Conscious knowledge of the opposing luciferic and ahrimanic forces is needed; otherwise, the consciousness soul will not develop completely. The human being is exposed to these powers and challenged to seek a balance in life between the two opposing powers. In our time there must be a significant effort to reach a balance, although the balance is never permanent but always in danger of veering off to one side or the other. In passing through these experiences of the consciousness soul, the human being inwardly develops the Spirit Self. In Rudolf Steiner's words:

As it develops, the Spirit Self will work socially to the same degree that the consciousness soul works antisocially. Thus we can say that the human being is developing an antisocial element out of the inmost impulses of his soul in the present time; but a spiritual, social factor is at work behind the antisocial element.[4]

Rudolf Steiner's indication of a social law for our own time can be understood in this sense. He says:

To the extent human beings permeate their souls with a recognition of the spiritual element I have described today, so that all that is spiritual in the age also flows down into their consciousness—to that extent a normal life of community can develop in humanity; to that extent human beings can get beyond their antisocial drives, beyond everything that works against socialization.[5]

From the above it becomes clear that the 'we' in the last part of the Foundation Stone can be related to the powers of the Spirit Self. It does not indicate an old group soul element, but something new that can arise as the human being turns to the spirit.

The Rhythms of the Foundation Stone and the Members of the Human Constitution

In the echo of my inner work with the Foundation Stone's rhythms, it became evident to me that the members of the human constitution find expression in these rhythms. My attempt to trace this inner result does not represent an effort to prove something; I have simply sought to explain how the seven rhythms might be viewed as an expression of the seven members of the human being. Thus this discussion is only a provisional one.

I will begin by mentioning two fields of inner work where this relationship to the members of the human being can be established or traced. These two inner fields are: the conditions for esoteric schooling and the subsidiary exercises. The chapter on 'The Conditions for Esoteric Schooling' in *Knowledge of the Higher Worlds and its Attainment* notes seven conditions that are important for the esoteric student.[6] In working with these conditions, it is possible to feel their connection with the members of the human being. The first condition is that esoteric students pay attention to their physical and spiritual health; this is clearly connected with the physical body. The second condition is to feel oneself a part of all life; this is related to the etheric body of the human being. The third condition calls up the insight that thoughts and feelings are as important to the world as are deeds; this is directly related to the astral body. The fourth condition concerns the development of a 'spiritual balance' between the inner world and the outer world; this is connected to the I of the human being. The fifth condition has to do with perseverance in following through on a decision once made; this leads to the area of the Spirit Self. The spiritual student begins to act out of love for the deed; it is the beginning of service in sacrifice. The sixth condition is connected with developing a feeling of gratitude in regard to all that is given to the human being; this feeling of gratitude arises when our own existence is felt as a gift of the entire universe. Here we enter the sphere of the Life Spirit. The seventh condition is always to live our lives in keeping with the previous six conditions; this brings the spiritual student into the sphere of the Spirit-man.

The so-called subsidiary exercises represent a second field that is related to the members of the human being. Rudolf Steiner points to this connection in two lessons of the Esoteric School given in 1914.[7] In an esoteric lesson held a year and a half earlier, Rudolf Steiner had indicated the purpose of the subsidiary exercises.[8] Those who carefully perform the subsidiary exercises will notice that they are beginning to develop in morality. I will briefly indicate here the connection between the subsidiary exercises and the members of the human constitution. In the first subsidiary exercise, that of concentration, a strengthening of the thinking arises; thus the human being is in a position to take possession of the physical body so that there is a freer relationship to it. Through the second exercise, the exercise of will in connection with the intent of one's actions, the human being learns to feel the presence of the etheric body, to feel the etheric body awaken. In the third exercise, that of composure, the human being meets his astral body; he learns to feel how the outer astral world meets the inner astral world. The composure that arises in this exercise allows for a freer relationship with this process. With the fourth exercise, the development of a positive viewpoint, the human being learns to enter as a spiritual I into the being and substance of all things through the power of love. This spiritual I then looks back at the individual from all creation. Through the fifth exercise, that of objectivity, hidden wisdom, as Spirit Self, can stream from the spiritual world towards the human being as a gift of grace. These five steps lead to contact with the spiritual world. The sixth exercise is harmony in the interplay of the five preceding exercises. One of Rudolf Steiner's descriptions draws attention to the fact that further exercises reach even higher; we can think of the sphere of the Life Spirit and that of the Spirit Man. (I will not go here into the formation of the twelve-petalled lotus flower in the heart region as described in *Knowledge of the Higher Worlds*.)

Based on these relationships, the seven rhythms of the Foundation Stone Meditation can be characterized as expressive of the seven members of the human being.

After noting in the Christmas Foundation Meeting on Tuesday, 25 December 1923 that the Foundation Stone has a connection with the threefold nature of the human being, Rudolf Steiner begins on Wednesday, 26 December 1923 with the rhythms of the mantra. He starts the first rhythm by writing the three words 'spirit-recalling', 'spirit-contemplating' and 'spirit-beholding' on the blackboard. Then written below 'spirit-recalling' are the words 'Your own I within the I of God arises—.' Below 'spirit-contemplating' he added the words 'Your own I unto the I of the World unite—.' Under 'spirit-beholding', 'On your own I for your free willing bestow—.' Rudolf Steiner adds that it is important to feel the moral element in the verb transitions from 'arises' to 'unite' to 'bestow.' It is striking that the verb 'practise' is missing from the 'spirit-recalling,' 'spirit-contemplating' and 'spirit-beholding' on the board. It seems that a certain fact is being indicated at first, a fact that has not yet become active. Your own I can be experienced as arising within the I of God in the spirit-recalling that takes place in the depths of the soul. Likewise, in the spirit-contemplating that reveals itself in balance of the soul there is an experience of how the surging deeds of world-evolving continually renew the union between your own I and the I of the World. Finally, in the spirit-beholding contained within the stillness of a life in thought it is possible to grasp how your own I constantly receives the gift of light for your free willing. Through a continuing awareness of the facts of his incarnation, the human being establishes an accurate relationship with the current nature of his physical body.

On Thursday, 27 December 1923 Rudolf Steiner writes the second rhythm on the board. Three aspects of the I are noted through the grammar of the German original: in the first strophe, the I acts; in the second strophe, the I is acted upon; and in the third strophe, the I receives light, enabling it to act in a free way. Then the words 'live', 'feel', and 'think' are added to their respective strophes as an expression of the inner soul situation. Finally the phrases 'human being of worlds', 'human work of soul', and 'human depths of spirit' are added. Keep in mind that this is still the first part of the first, second and third strophes, the so-called microcosmic part. However, through the activities of living, feeling and thinking it is possible to experience a connection with the etheric constitution of the human being. These activities connect him to his etheric surroundings — this is expressed in phrases coined by Rudolf Steiner: 'human being of worlds', 'human work of soul' and 'human depths of spirit'.

On Friday, 28 December 1923 a connection is made for the first time between the first and second parts of the three strophes. Not only do we find 'spirit-recalling', 'spirit-contemplating', and 'spirit-beholding', but they are now preceded by the verb 'practise.' There is to be an inner activation of recalling, meditating and beholding. Through this activation a relationship arises between the first, microcosmic part and the second, macrocosmic part of the first, second and third strophes. Thus the following is written on the board for each of the three strophes: 'practise spirit-recalling — For the Father-Spirit of the heights reigns in depths of worlds begetting being'; 'practise spirit-contemplating — For the Christ-will reigns in the encircling round, gracing souls in rhythms of worlds'; and 'practise spirit-beholding — For the Spirit's World-thoughts reign in being of worlds, imploring light'. The addition of the verb 'practise' makes it clear that an inner activity is needed if these forces that reign in the universe are to become effective. The human being needs these forces for work on the astral body. An indirect path is indicated here. The forces do not work directly; they work in sleep when the astral body and the I are freed of the physical and etheric bodies. These are forces of the Trinity towards which every human being has an inner inclination, an inclination often denied in our time. Rudolf Steiner indicates that this denial causes illness in relation to the body, a fateful unhappiness in relation to the soul, and a dullness in relation to the spirit.[9] Work on the astral body can only take place in the right way when forces from beyond the threshold, forces from the spiritual world, have an effect in the astral body. This happens in sleep when the human being has cultivated his inclination for the forces of the Trinity through a sharpened focus of attention during the day. This heightened attention, this soul-spirit awakening, is brought forth by the threefold practice of spirit-recalling, spirit-contemplating and spirit-beholding. During the night, from the time we go to sleep to the time we awake, the astral body is suffused with colour according to its moral feelings; it then becomes the 'judge' of the human soul.[10]

On Saturday, 29 December 1923 the three practices are written on the board, followed by the initials of the hierarchies in each. Then, below the first hierarchy, 'Let ring from the heights what in the depths is echoed'; below the second, 'Let from the east be enkindled what through the west receives form;' and below the third, 'Let from the depths be entreated what in the heights will be heard'. Here the focus is the I of the human being that can find its pure expression in the consciousness soul. Rudolf Steiner explains that the Christ-being brought the great impulse of the macrocosmic I so that the microcosmic I, the human I, could take up this impulse and thereby make progress in its evolution.[11] Taking up the macrocosmic I makes it possible to spiritualize the human soul. On this basis, and in the practice of spirit-recalling, spirit-contemplating and spirit-beholding, the human being can establish a connection with the beings of the hierarchies. This connection is real in deep sleep. Then we share something with the beings of the higher hierarchies in the world of Intuition. We are in that world where karma becomes reality for us, where our destiny unfolds from earth life to earth life.[12] These beings also play a role in developing different phases of destiny in human life. Rudolf Steiner indicates that the I of the human being receives effects from many sources:

> Seen outwardly, they are the effects of the mineral, the plant, the animal elements; seen inwardly, seen in respect to the spiritual–soul element, they are the effects of the third hierarchy—the angeloi, the archangeloi, the archai; the effects of the second hierarchy—the exusiai, the dynameis, the kyriotetes; the effects of the first hierarchy—the seraphim, the cherubim, the thrones.[13]

In the chapter 'On Repeated Earth Lives and Karma' found in *The Threshold of the Spiritual World*, Rudolf Steiner says that supersensible consciousness learns to say 'I' to the whole of destiny in the same way that the physical person says 'I' to his own being. What we call karma merges with the spiritual I-being. Behind the course of a human being's life stands the inspiration brought by his own permanent nature that continues from life to life.[14]

On Sunday, 30 December 1923 a further important step is

taken. First, Rudolf Steiner writes the three practices next to one another on the board. Then he writes the last part of the fourth strophe under them. The fourth strophe begins with an indication that the macrocosmic I entered the stream of earth existence at the turning point of time and thereby made possible a new development of humanity. Thanks to this unique event, a spiritualization of the human soul can occur. With this internalization, the human being can open up to the light of the spirit. This light gleams forth within the I. The human being himself becomes an expression of the spirit; he develops the Spirit Self. Rudolf Steiner makes this process concrete in relation to the social element as follows:

> A peculiar characteristic of the age of the consciousness soul is that the human being receives his I only as a mirror image. Thus he is enabled to live his way into the age of the Spirit Self and reshape his I; he is enabled to experience his I in a new form. But he will experience this I very differently from the way he would prefer to experience it at present! Today, the human being would prefer to call his I, which he experiences only as a mirror image, something other than what he will find presented to him as an I in the sixth post-Atlantean epoch of the future. Those mystical fits people still have today — introspective brooding to find their true I which they even call their divine I — such fits will become rarer for people in the future. But they will have to get used to seeing this I only in the outer world. The strange situation will arise that others who meet us and become involved with us will have more connection with our I than anything enclosed within our own skin. Thus the human being has set his course for the social age. In the future he will tell himself: 'My self is in everything that

comes to meet me from without; it is hardly to be found within.'[15]

This lends the 'we' in the Foundation Stone Meditation a special depth. As noted above, Rudolf Steiner indicates this situation concisely in the sentence: 'As it develops, the Spirit Self will work socially to the same degree that the consciousness soul works antisocially.'

In this rhythm, the three practices are no longer individually connected with the second, macrocosmic portion of the first three strophes. They are connected as a whole with the last part of the fourth strophe. This states, 'What we found from our hearts and direct from our heads with focused will,' so that it will become good. Now the practice of spirit-recalling, spirit-contemplating and spirit-beholding relates directly to our activity in waking life. In the process it becomes possible to strive for three ideals. Those are the ideals of the fifth post-Atlantean epoch: human social understanding (or brotherhood for our bodies) through spirit-recalling, freedom of thought (or religious freedom for the soul) through spirit-contemplating and spiritual knowledge (or spiritual science for the spirit) through spirit-beholding.[16] The sixth post-Atlantean epoch is being prepared through these activities; we become co-responsible for this development towards the good.

On Monday, 31 December 1923 Rudolf Steiner begins with the following words on the board: 'Light divine, Chr.-Sun.' Then he writes the words of the ending for the first, second and third strophes: 'This is heard by the spirits of the elements in the E. [east], W. [west], N. [north], S. [south]: May human beings hear it!' Here it becomes clear that the divine light of the Christ-Sun has begun its work in the etheric world, and that the spirits of the elements hear it! In this rhythm, the verb 'hear' is used, a verb that occurs in connection with the verb 'speaking' in the first three strophes of the mantra. Its use here means that the inner Word and thus the inner sense of things can resound in the ether body of the human being.

> This inner sounding, which is of course not a sounding perceptible to the outer, sensory ear, this inner Word of things in which they express their own nature — that is the experience the human being has when he is able to work from his astral body to affect his ether body.[17]

It is the etheric sphere that now begins to sound and be heard by the spirits of the elements. It is the sphere where the Resurrected One has begun to work. The etheric spirit of the human being, or the bodily member of the Life Spirit, is being developed in this sphere.[18]

On Tuesday, 1 January 1924, the last day of the Christmas Foundation Meeting, Rudolf Steiner writes the first words from the first strophe following the call 'Human soul' on the board. Then he continues with the first words of the second part of the first strophe. These are followed by the corresponding words of the second and third strophes. This expresses the fact that the microcosm and the macrocosm are in complete harmony. The human being has built up a spiritual body within the spiritual world. He has become a Spirit Man within the spiritual world. This reality can also be viewed as follows: through the one-time event of the Christ's resurrection in the spiritual atmosphere of the earth, a complete human phantom, a human body raised from the grave, has been and continues to be there as a supersensible form. This spirit body can reproduce like a seed and be passed on to all human beings.[19]

'We' as an Expression of a Spirit Self Quality

From the above it can be understood that the fifth rhythm, the Sunday rhythm, is lent a special quality. The 'we' is no ordinary 'we;' it can be grasped as the expression of a Spirit Self quality. Another special light is thrown on this 'we' in the karma lectures that follow the Christmas Foundation Meeting. There, Rudolf Steiner begins to speak about the karma of the Anthroposophical Society.[20] The next section represents an attempt to consider this 'we' from a karmic standpoint.

Part Two

Rules and Exceptions in Karmic Relationships

In a June 1924 lecture in Breslau, Rudolf Steiner indicates that people who are led to one another during one earth life seek to find each other in the next earth life as well. As a rule, we continually meet people on the earth who had been incarnated with us before. Rudolf Steiner closes his observation with the comment that this insight (i.e., in the course of earth's evolution people live together in groups) is the rule, but that everything is individual in the spirit. As an example, he cites his geometry teacher whose karma clearly shows that the general rule about people passing through their earth lives in groups has been broken. In this connection, he says that it is the exception that makes the significance of this rule clear.[21]

At the beginning of July 1924, Rudolf Steiner emphasizes that the spiritualization the Anthroposophical Society has striven for since the Christmas Meeting requires us to become increasingly conscious of the spiritual and cosmic basis for a community like the Anthroposophical Society. It then becomes possible for the individual to find his place in the Society with this consciousness. Thus Rudolf Steiner begins to speak about the karma of the Anthroposophical Society, quite a complicated one as a general karma arising through the karmic confluence of many individual human beings.[22]

In the first lecture in Arnheim[23] he makes it clear that the Michael stream generally consists of two groups of souls who had not been incarnated together until the twentieth century; he then speaks about the special destiny of the Anthroposophical Society. This destiny is that many of those connected with the Anthroposophical Society at the beginning of the twentieth century will again be on the earth at the close of the century and will be united then with those who were in the School of Chartres. The Platonists of Chartres and the later Aristotelians were to work together on the earth before the end of the twentieth century.

This breaks the rule that, karmically speaking, human beings incarnate in groups. Rudolf Steiner's indication about this working together leads to the thought that the 'we' in the Foundation Stone Meditation has a quality that differentiates it from a single, defined karmic group. Rudolf Steiner confirms this in Torquay during the summer of 1924. There he indicates that the particular form taken by the Michael regency will lead to the following: those personalities who now (i.e. at that time) join the anthroposophical movement — breaking many of the laws of reincarnation in the process — will be reincarnated at the turn of the twentieth into the twenty-first century in order to bring to a culmination, to full expression, what they now (i.e. at the beginning of the twentieth century) are able to do in anthroposophical service to the Michael regency.[24] Finally, in September 1924, Rudolf Steiner says:

> Those human beings who honestly take up anthroposophy today are preparing their souls to appear again at the end of the twentieth century, with the briefest possible time between death and a new birth. They will then be united with the teachers from Chartres who have remained behind.[25]

In his last Dornach lecture before his trip to England in the summer of 1924, Rudolf Steiner repeats his indication that the cosmic intelligence has descended into the individual human being. He then asks, 'Just what is this intelligence?' and answers with the words, 'The mutual rules of behaviour among the higher hierarchies are cosmic intelligence. What they do, how they behave with one another, how they relate to one another—that is cosmic intelligence.' He describes how some angel beings separated from the Michael realm where they had been earlier. The one angel belonging to two karmically connected human souls remained with Michael; the other angel went down to earth, became a terrestrial angel. Rudolf Steiner then asks: 'What had to happen then?' And he answers that the karma of human beings fell into disorder after the year 869 as a result. Disorder has entered the karma of modern humanity. His question 'What unites the members of the Anthroposophical Society?' is answered briefly and decisively:

> What unites them is that they are to bring their karma into order! ... That is the karmic ray that pours through the anthroposophical movement for the person who recognizes it: restoring the truth of karma.

Rudolf Steiner closes this lecture with the statement that there is an overall truth in karmic relationships and the cosmic exceptions now need to be brought back into alignment with these rules. This is the task, the mission, of the anthroposophical movement.[26]

Events in the Ninth Century

Then comes the trip to England where Rudolf Steiner describes much more fully the events taking place in the spiritual world in 869 while on the earth the Eighth General

Ecumenical Council was being held in Constantinople. It was at this Council that the trichotomy (the view that the human being consists of body, soul and spirit) was condemned as heretical. Harun-al-Rashid and his advisor met with Alexander the Great and Aristotle in the spiritual world. The old spirituality of Alexandrism and Aristotelianism had persisted at the court of Harun-al-Rashid in isolation from the events surrounding the Mystery of Golgotha. At the time of the Mystery of Golgotha, the individualities, the souls, of Alexander and Aristotle were not on the earth but in the spiritual world where they were intimately connected with the regency of Michael. They saw the Christ take his leave of the sun, and they took up the impulse of doing what they could to help the new Michael regency institute an intensive form of Christianity. Neither Harun-al-Rashid nor his wise advisor wanted to hear of this. A spiritual battle took place that has its effects even today.[27] Then, in London, Rudolf Steiner describes a simultaneous meeting in the spiritual world between the Christ who had gone through the Mystery of Golgotha, and His image, His Life Spirit. The Christ, who had descended through the Mystery of Golgotha and entered into the hearts of human beings, meets His spiritual, etheric image that had remained behind in the circumference of the earth as the Christ descended from the sun. It is the meeting between the Christ and His own self, between the Christ as the Brother of human beings and the Christ as the Sun Hero, now present only as an image. This meeting is reflected on the earth in the meeting between the Grail stream and the Arthurian stream.[28]

During his last lecture in Torquay, Rudolf Steiner notes that as these three simultaneous events took place, human beings were also beginning to develop their own intelligence in the ninth century; in a sense, they were paving the way for humanity as a whole. They begin to grasp in their own souls the intelligence that had been administered as cosmic intelligence by Michael up to then. This was perceived by Michael and his followers as they looked down from the sun to the earth. They saw how sovereignty over intelligence was slowly falling away from them. Thus, during the next Michael regency (from the year 1879 onwards), it resolved to rediscover the intelligence that had fallen from heaven to earth, and to administer it in the hearts, the souls, of human beings. Rudolf Steiner then says that Michael will want to establish his abode in the hearts, in the souls, of human beings on the earth in the future. This is to begin in the Michael Age, an age that is also to lead Christianity to deeper truths.[29] Cosmic intelligence descends and, at the same time, the karma of human beings begins to fall into disarray.[30] Here we find a connection between intelligence and karma, one that begins with these three events in the ninth century. This relationship will be discussed later.

Events in the Fourth Century

Something had taken place in the spiritual world during the fourth century to prepare for the descent of intelligence to the earth: the thoughts spread throughout the cosmos as the universal forces that rule the world were passed on from the Exusiai (the beings of form) to the Archai (the primal powers or primal beginnings). A fundamental shift in the human soul begins with this event; human beings feel themselves more centered in their individuality. As the world of thoughts passes from the beings of form to the primal beginnings, from the Exusiai to the Archai who are one step closer to human beings, people become more strongly aware of their own thoughts. However, certain spirits of form could not bring themselves to hand their powers of thought over to the primal beginnings; they kept them for themselves. This made human beings vulnerable in the following way: Someone with a suitable karma receives the impulses of his thinking through the archai; thus his thinking, his thoughts—even the objective ones—become his personal possession. Others have not yet reached the point of working out their thoughts as a personal possession. They accept their thoughts either as a legacy from their parents and ancestors or they adopt traditional thoughts derived from membership in a particular group. This event involving the powers of thought lays the foundation for inner human freedom, for the possibility that the individual human being can act out of himself, a possibility that was not to become a reality until the age of the consciousness soul.[31] But here we see the point where the sense of having a group soul begins to diminish; it is a change that affects karma itself.

A process Rudolf Steiner described in Penmaenmawr during the summer of 1923 should also be viewed in the light of this fourth-century event.[32] There is a point in the evolution of the world and humanity through which humanity must pass as it leaves behind the earlier determination of its being by external forces and becomes more and more able to find its way towards the conscious, individual acquisition of higher levels of knowledge—and its ultimate goal of freedom. This point is found around the year 333 after the birth of the Christ. That is when the upper and lower parts of the human astral body come into balance. Previously, the upper part was larger than the lower part—that is how higher divine-spiritual beings were able to influence the human being. An equilibrium is established in 333, a critical development for the evolution of humanity. The upper part of the human astral body has been growing smaller ever since. This is the precondition for the development of the I in the human being. If this waning of the upper part of the astral body had not taken place, the I would not have had a strong enough effect to bring about human freedom. But as the upper part of the astral body diminished, all of humanity also began to fall ill. This tendency towards illness can be overcome only through the strengthening of the I that radiates from the Mystery of Golgotha.

It is striking that this great crisis arises approximately in the year 333, the exact middle of the fourth cultural epoch during which the intellectual soul was being developed. It also marks the midpoint between the birth of the Christ and the point when the academy of Gondishapur mounted a powerful attempt in 666 to bring human beings the culture of the consciousness soul, and soul-spiritual achievements connected with it, prematurely. An inappropriate juncture of the intellectual soul and the consciousness soul was intended. The consciousness soul was to be artificially injected into the human being in the seventh century, thus cutting this soul off from the development of the Spirit Self, the Life Spirit, and the Spirit Man. Humanity was to be instilled with something it was not supposed to achieve until the middle of the consciousness soul period (i.e. in the year 2493), and only after a long process of maturation: the knowledge of birth and death (eugenic occultism), knowledge of the course of life (hygienic occultism) and knowledge of nature (mechanical occultism).[33] All of these require a high degree of truth, conscientiousness and social responsibility, values not to be developed until the age of the consciousness soul when the inner maturity necessary for this knowledge is present. These values are also connected with the three ideals of the fifth post-Atlantean cultural period mentioned earlier.

The Mystery of Death and of Evil

With the Mystery of Golgotha, a healthy, I-related development of mankind had become possible. The Mystery of Golgotha was a deed of free will—i.e. of love—so that the earth and humanity could reach their goal.[34] The Christ worked less through His teachings and more through what He did. The greatest deed of the Christ was that He passed through death. Significant here is that the Christ performed a deed that had its effect in the world after He was no longer physically present. And this deed affects only those human beings who make a decision to let it work upon them; it is compatible with the absolutely free quality of their I. To accept the Christ is a free decision by the human I.[35] Here we should remember that of all the beings in world evolution, it is only the human being on the physical plane who can experience death. A central task for human beings is overcoming death. But the human being also develops his I-consciousness on the physical plane. He could not find this I-consciousness without the death he experiences on the physical plane. The Christ-being—so closely connected with the development of I-consciousness—enacts the Mystery of Golgotha as His most significant deed on earth: overcoming death through life. Among all the important deeds for our life as a higher being, it is only the death on Golgotha that can be understood solely within the physical body. If an understanding for this is achieved on the physical plane, that understanding can then be developed further in the higher worlds.[36]

There are two mysteries with special significance in the development of humanity during the age of the consciousness soul: the mystery of death and the mystery of evil. The mystery of death involves the forces in the universe that endow the human being with a full capacity for the consciousness soul. As the earth develops, the human being must take these forces of death into his own being so that he can acquire a capacity for the consciousness soul. The forces of evil work in another way on the human being; they seize upon a part of his being. In looking for the evil in human beings, it is not enough merely to look at their evil deeds; their evil tendencies must also be taken into account. Then it becomes clear that evil tendencies, evil proclivities, have been present in the subconscious of every human being since the beginning of the fifth post-Atlantean period. The entry of the human being into the fifth post-Atlantean period is marked by the fact that he takes this propensity for evil into himself. He must discover this propensity within his own soul if he is to plant any kind of inner seed that leads to an experience of spiritual substance with the consciousness soul. The forces of evil are there so that the human being can break through to a spiritual life on the level of the consciousness soul. If the human being had not taken this inclination for evil into himself, he could never reach the point where he received the spirit out of the cosmos by means of his consciousness soul. Through evil, humanity is led to a renewal of the Mystery of Golgotha. The experience of evil makes it possible for the Christ to reappear.[37] It is clear that the mystery of death and the mystery of evil are connected to the development of the consciousness soul. These two mysteries have within them a deep responsibility for the contribution the modern human being is to make to the evolution of the world.

The Second Crucifixion and Resurrection

Rudolf Steiner's 1913 statements in London about a second crucifixion on the etheric plane are significant in this regard. He begins by indicating that the most central element in the Mystery of Golgotha is that the Christ passed through death. There is no death in the spiritual world, only transformation of consciousness. The passage of the Christ-being through the experience of death forged an inner bond between earthly humanity and the Christ. Since then the Christ has lived in the souls of human beings on earth, and He experiences life on earth with them. Thus the earth received its meaning through the Mystery of Golgotha. Then Rudolf Steiner indicates that the Christ-being can be recognized again in one of the beings belonging to the hierarchy of the Angels. The angel-being that has been the outer form of the Christ since the Mystery of Golgotha suffered an extinction of consciousness during the nineteenth century, the result of materialistic forces carried up into the spiritual world by human souls that bore the imprint of materialism as they passed through the gate of death. From the sixteenth century on, more and more darkness arose from 'the seeds of earthly materialism' carried up to the spiritual world in ever-increasing quantities by souls passing through the gate of death; these seeds formed 'the black sphere of materialism'. In keeping with the Manichaean principle, the Christ took this black sphere into his own being in order to transform it. It brought about a 'spiritual death by suffocation' in the angel-being that had been the revelation of the Christ-being since the Mystery of Golgotha.

This sacrifice of the Christ in the nineteenth century is comparable to the sacrifice on the physical plane that came with the Mystery of Golgotha; it can be called the second crucifixion of the Christ on the etheric plane. The second death by suffocation leading to an obliteration of consciousness in that angel-being is a repetition of the Mystery of Golgotha in the worlds lying directly behind our own; this repetition makes it possible for a Christ consciousness to be resurrected in the souls of human beings on earth, a resurrection that becomes humanity's clairvoyant envisioning in the twentieth century. Rudolf Steiner states:

> The Christ has been crucified twice: once physically in the physical world at the beginning of our era, and a second time spiritually in the nineteenth century as described. We might say that humanity experienced the resurrection of His body earlier, and will experience the resurrection of His consciousness from the twentieth century on.

The mediator, the messenger, of this event will be Michael as the emissary of the Christ.[38]

Rudolf Steiner's unique reference to the second crucifixion of the Christ on the etheric plane can bring the nature of the age in which we live as humanity to consciousness. We carry our full share of responsibility for events that take place in the spiritual world.

A Free-will Deed

In Arnheim, Rudolf Steiner uses cosmic-imaginative language to describe how the souls connected with Michael and united on the sun see the Christ departing to unite Himself with the course of earth evolution.[39] The Christ left the sun to connect His destiny with the destiny of humanity. 'He is going forth!' was the great experience. A mighty impulse arose at the cosmic moment in world history when these souls saw the Christ going forth from the sun. And at the same time they understood: Now the cosmic intelligence is gradually passing from the cosmos to the earth. The Christ-being performed this deed out of free will — that is, out of love. The result was that intelligence also fell to the earth. This put Michael into the peculiar position of no longer being able to participate in earthly matters from the sun. His age-old activity — the administration of cosmic intelligence — now came to an end. Thus, as Rudolf Steiner tells us in the words of Michael to his followers, it became 'necessary to find a special task, a task within the region of the sun, for the period when we cannot send our impulses to the earth, the period that will end approximately in the year 1879'. Then Rudolf Steiner describes how an entirely new way of working arose in the region of the sun under Michael's regency, now freed of earthly matters. A supersensible school formed under the leadership of Michael. Although Rudolf Steiner does not go further into this deed of Michael, we might understand from it that Michael, as a follower of the Christ, also performed a free-will deed.

If we now think of what happened at the 1923–24 Christmas Foundation Meeting — where this supersensible school found its earthly home as the School for Spiritual Science within the newly founded General Anthroposophical Society — and if we call Rudolf Steiner's deed to mind, we can sense that Rudolf Steiner was performing an act of free will at the Christmas meeting. These three events give us a feeling for the new Christ–Michael power that would work karmically within humanity.

Rudolf Steiner characterizes Michael's nature as one that reveals nothing to the human being who does not work hard spiritually to bring Michael something from the earth. He says:

> Michael is a silent spirit. Michael is a being who keeps his own counsel. While other reigning archangels are loquacious spirits — in a spiritual sense, of course — Michael is a wholly taciturn spirit, a spirit who says little, one who will give sparse indications at most. For what one experiences from Michael, in fact, is not the word, but — if I may say so — the gaze, the power of the gaze. And this is because Michael is actually most involved with what human beings create out of the spiritual element. He lives in the effects of what human beings create. The other spirits live more in the causes. Michael lives more in the effects. The other spirits motivate the human being to do what ought to be done. Michael will be the truly spiritual hero of freedom. He allows human beings to act, but takes up what results from human deeds in order to extend it in the cosmos, in order to make effective in the cosmos what human beings are not yet able to accomplish.[40]

The period of the consciousness soul for which Michael is the time spirit began in 1879. This period is unique and will last about 350 years. It is unique because the human being needs to find a responsible connection with the events of our time out of his own initiative, i.e. in freedom. Thus the destiny of our time can become the destiny of our own soul. At present we live in the transition from the first third of this period to the second, middle third. We are entering the middle of the Michael age. This is an age when it is especially important 'that an anthroposophist's soul should always have before it, written in golden letters, that taking initiative is in his karma'.[41] The age of Michael is a time when our karma is inscribed with the words 'Become a person who takes initiative.' To find initiatives of soul, to be able to start something out of our inmost being, to be able to make a decision—these are the things that are asked of us now more than ever.

Restoring the Truth of Karma

In his last Dornach lecture before setting off to England in the summer of 1924, Rudolf Steiner not only indicates what the cosmic intelligence is—the way the hierarchies relate to one another—but also that there is always a certain tension between the intelligence of the planets and the sun intelligence. The sun intelligence stood under the regency of Michael, and the six planetary intelligences under the regency of the other archangels—each of whom led a period of about 350 years in the development of mankind. The individual beings from the archangelic hierarchy were co-regents of the cosmic intelligence, but Michael always reigned over them as the administrator of cosmic intelligence as a whole. There was a change in the ninth century—the other planetary intelligences no longer wished to be ruled by the sun. They decided that the earth should not continue to be dependent on the sun, but should be directly dependent on the cosmos as a whole. The planetary decisions of the archangels led to this. Under the leadership of Oriphiel, the planetary intelligences emancipated themselves from the sun intelligence. There was a complete separation of the cosmic powers that had belonged together up to then. The sun intelligence of Michael and the planetary intelligences gradually came to oppose one another. The angelic beings perceived this split in the life of the planets and had to decide which direction to take. As we have noted, the result was a split among the angels, the beings who participate in forming our karmic development. Thus the karma of humanity fell into disorder.

Rudolf Steiner then indicates that a power began to radiate from Michael with the beginning of the Michael regency in 1879, one that can restore order to the karma of those who have remained with him.[42] What Michaelic power is meant here? Based on our previous discussion, it seems clear that a renewed power of intelligence is meant, one that can work once again in a Michaelic–cosmic way. It is power that overcomes intellectuality and involves the entire human being. This power can only be developed out of free initiative. It is the power of ethical individualism in the sense of Rudolf Steiner's *Philosophy of Freedom*.[43]

On the one hand, the Michael stream described by Rudolf Steiner in his karma lectures has its karmic causes; on the other, it is expressed as a true Michael stream only when karma is brought into order. An important event in this connection is that the Christ becomes the Lord of Karma for humanity's development towards the end of the twentieth century (i.e. in the present time). Karmic circumstances are being brought into order by the Christ. This means that karmic balance is being woven in the best possible way into the general context of the cosmos. Christ will fit our karmic balance into the karma of the earth as a whole, into the progress of humanity as a whole.[44] Thus it is clear that those gathered together in the Anthroposophical Society can achieve a karma-ordering communality only if they can bring this Christ event to full realization within their souls. It should also be noted that during the preparations for the 1923–24 Christmas Foundation Conference, Rudolf Steiner called attention to the following spiritual law: every spiritual movement that truly advances mankind must be there for all of humanity.[45] Through the Anthroposophical Society a 'we' can be created in the sense of the Foundation Stone Meditation, one without any trace of a group soul, a 'we' that has a genuinely human character.

At the close of his last address—which opens a new dimension in his work—Rudolf Steiner indicates that light will pour over humanity through the Michael stream and Michael deeds if the Michael thought becomes fully alive in at least 4 times 12 human beings.[46] Here the number 4 can be connected with the four great cosmic directions called upon at the close of the first three strophes. The number 12 evokes Rudolf Steiner's reference to the twelve members of King Arthur's Round Table as he spoke about the way in which karmic relations between people were brought into balance.[47] The new dimension touched upon in the last address has to do especially with the incarnation series of Elijah, Lazarus–John, Raphael, and Novalis; John the Baptist is missing here. The soul of John the Baptist— which is also the soul of Elijah—becomes the group soul of the twelve apostles after the Baptist is beheaded; it lives on in the twelve. This allows the twelve to achieve a higher understanding, a process that can be seen as a kind of preparation for the heightening of the powers of intelligence that can arise today in such groups of twelve.[48] Here one can get a sense for Rudolf Steiner's intimation that when cosmic intelligence has become our own intelligence it can work between people so that it becomes cosmic intelligence once again, but now permeated by the human being. Then 'we' can become participants in helping to bring about what anthroposophy is meant to accomplish for earthly development in a Michaelic way.

Thus we arrive at closing thoughts that lead back to the Foundation Stone. The first three strophes consist of two parts, a microcosmic and a macrocosmic part. The first part of each relates to the human being; the second, to the world. With the fourth strophe it becomes possible to give karmic form to the relationship between the human being and the world. The Christ, as the macrocosmic I-Being, enters the stream of earth existence. The impulses from the macrocosmic I can be taken up by the human being, the microcosmic I, because there is an intimate relationship between the human I and the cosmic I.[49] Thus we find ourselves on a path of transformation. An inward turning of the soul makes possible what 'we' would found from our hearts, and a humanization of intelligence makes possible what 'we' would direct from our heads, so that karmically good may become what 'we' intend, what 'we' do. In this way we work at restoring the truth of karma. The 'we' arises on this path of transformation. It is neither group-specific nor a fiction; it is inspired by the I and open to the world; it forms the connection between human being and world in a karmically real way. This is not only a deed for the human realm; it is also a deed for the realm of the Angels.

The Foundation Stone Meditation

With the words spoken by Rudolf Steiner at the close of the
Christmas Foundation Meeting, 1 January 1924

This is why we have gone so deeply into those words with which we began; into those words with which I would like to close this Christmas meeting, this Christmas meeting that should be a Christmas, a festival of consecration, for us — not just a new year, but the beginning of a cosmic turning point in time to which we would dedicate ourselves in devoted care for the life of the spirit.

> Human soul!
> You live in the limbs
> That bear you through the world of space
> Within the being of spirit ocean:
> Practise spirit-recalling
> In depths of soul,
> Where in the reigning
> World-Creator-Being,
> Your own I
> Within the I of God
> Arises,
> And you will truly live
> In human being of worlds.

> For the Father-Spirit of the heights reigns
> In depths of worlds begetting being.
> Seraphim, Cherubim, Thrones:
> Let ring from the heights

The Foundation Stone Meditation

What in the depths is echoed,
Speaking:
Ex deo nascimur
This is heard by the spirits of the elements
In east, west, north, south.
May human beings hear it!

Human soul!
You live within the beat of heart and lung
That leads you through the rhythms of time
Into the feeling of your own soul-being:
Practise spirit-contemplating
In balance of the soul,
Where the surging deeds
Of World-evolving
Your own I
Unto the I of the World
Unite,
And you will truly feel
In human work of soul.

For the Christ-will reigns in the encircling round,
Gracing souls in rhythms of worlds.
Kyriotetes, Dynameis, Exusiai:
Let from the east be enkindled
What through the west receives form,
Speaking:
In Christo morimur.
This is heard by the spirits of the elements
In east, west, north, south.
May human beings hear it!

Human soul!
You live within the resting head
Which from the grounds of eternity

Unlocks for you thoughts of worlds:
Practise spirit-beholding
In stillness of thought,
Where the eternal aims of gods
The light of World being,
For your free willing
On your own I
Bestow,
And you will truly think
In human depths of spirit.

For the Spirit's World-thoughts reign
In being of Worlds, imploring light.
Archai, Archangeloi, Angeloi:
Let from the depths be entreated
What in the heights will be heard,
Speaking:
Per spiritum sanctum reviviscimus.
[This is heard by the spirits of the elements
In east, west, north, south.
May human beings hear it!]

At the turning point of time
The Spirit-light of the world
Entered the stream of earth existence.
Darkness of night
Had ceased its reign;
Day-radiant light
Shone forth in human souls:
Light
That gives warmth
To simple shepherds' hearts;
Light
That enlightens
The wise heads of kings.

Light divine,
Christ-Sun,
Warm
Our hearts;
Enlighten
Our heads;
That good may become
What we found
From our hearts
And direct from our heads
With focused will.

So, my dear friends, carry your warm hearts out into the world, hearts into which you have laid the Foundation Stone for the Anthroposophical Society. Carry these warm hearts into the world so they may have a powerful effect, strong for healing. And you will receive help so that your heads enlighten by what each of you can direct with focused will. Today we resolve to do that with all our strength. And we shall see: If we show ourselves to be worthy, a good star will reign over what is willed from here. Follow this good star, my dear friends. We shall see where the gods will lead us through this star's light.

Light divine,
Christ-Sun,
Warm
Our hearts;
Enlighten
Our heads![50]

Spirit-Recalling	Spirit-Contemplating	Spirit-Beholding
○	○	○
Your own I	Your own I	Your own I
Within the I of God	Unto the I of the World	For your free Willing
Arises —	Unite —	Bestow —

26 December 1923

Your own I	Your own I	On your own I
Within the I of God	Unto the I of the World	For your free Willing
Arises	Unite	Bestow
Live	Feel	Think
Human Being of Worlds	Human Work of Soul	Human Depths of Spirit

27 December 1923

1

Practise Spirit-Recalling
For the Father Spirit of the Heights Reigns
In Depths of Worlds Begetting Being.

2

Practise Spirit-Contemplating
For the Christ-Will Reigns in the Encircling Round
Gracing Souls in Rhythms of Worlds.

3

Practise Spirit-Beholding
For the Spirit's World-Thoughts Reign
In Being of Worlds, Imploring Light.

28 December 1923

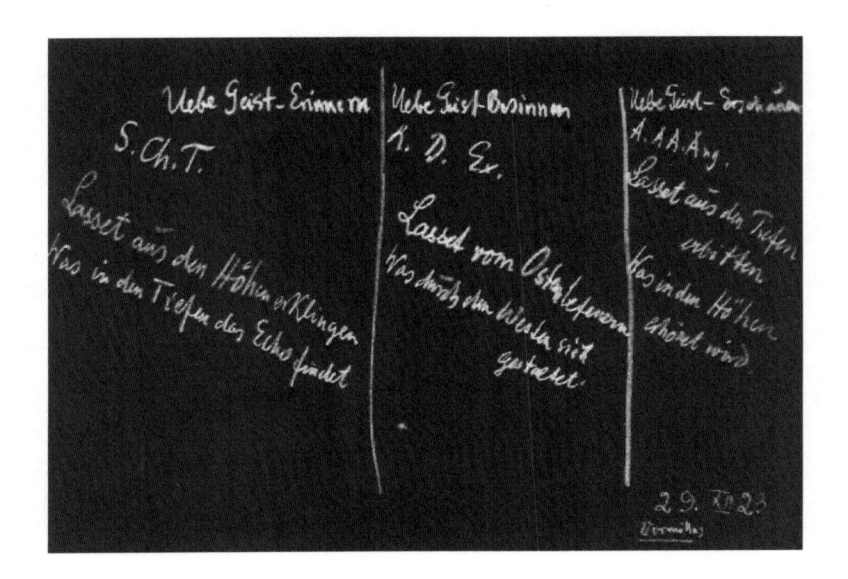

Practise Spirit-Recalling	Practise Spirit-Contemplating	Practise Spirit-Beholding
S. Ch. T.	K. D. Ex.	A. AA. Ang.
Let Ring from the Heights	Let from the East Be Enkindled	Let from the Depths Be Entreated
What in the Depths is Echoed	What through the West Receives Form	What in the Heights Will Be Heard

29 December 1923

                    Practise Spirit-Contemplating

 Spirit-Recalling   Practise Spirit-Beholding

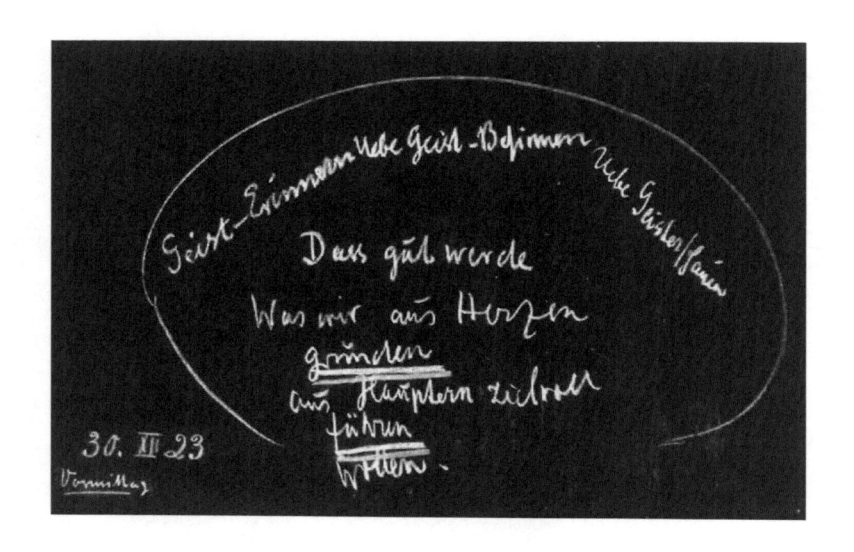

              That Good May Become
              What We Found from our
                       Hearts
               Direct from our Heads
                  With Focused Will

30 December 1923

Light Divine
Chr.—Sun
This Is Heard by the Spirits of the Elements
In
The E. W. N. S.
May Human Beings Hear It!

31 December 1923

You Live in the Limbs	You Live within the Beat of Heart and Lung
For the Father Spirit of the Heights Reigns	For the Christ-Will Reigns in the Encircling Round
In Depths of Worlds Begetting Being.	Gracing Souls in Rhythms of Worlds

You Live within the Resting Head
For the Spirit's World-Thoughts Reign
In Being of Worlds, Imploring Light

1 January 1924

Notes

For published titles in English translation see p. 49

1. *Freiheit und Gesellschaft* [Freedom and society] in *Magazin für Literatur* 67: 29–30 (1898); republished in *Gesammelte Aufsätze zur Kultur- und Zeitgeschichte 1887–1901* [Collected essays on cultural and contemporary history 1887–1901] (GA 31).
2. *Die soziale Grundforderung unserer Zeit – In geänderter Zeitlage* [The fundamental social need of our time – In a changed situation] (GA 186), lecture of 12 December 1918.
3. *Die Geschichte und Bedingungen der anthroposophischen Bewegung im Verhältnis zur Anthroposophischen Gesellschaft* [The history and limits of the anthroposophical movement in relation to the Anthroposophical Society] (GA 258), lecture of 16 June 1923.
4. *Soziale Grundforderungen* [Basic social requirements], lecture of 7 December 1918.
5. *Wie kann die Menschheit den Christus wiederfinden? Das dreifache Schattendasein unserer Zeit und das neue Christus-Licht* [How can humanity find the Christ again? The threefold shadow existence of our age and the new Christ-light] (GA 187), lecture of 1 January 1919.
6. *Wie erlangt man Erkenntnisse der höheren Welten?* [How does one acquire knowledge of higher worlds?] (GA 10).
7. *Aus den Inhalten der esoterischen Stunden* [From the contents of the esoteric lessons] (GA 266/3), Esoteric Lessons of 2 January 1914 and 7 February 1914.
8. Ibid., Esoteric Lesson of 7 June 1912.
9. *Der Tod als Lebenswandlung* [Death as a metamorphosis of life] (GA 182), lecture of 16 October 1918.
10. *Anthroposophie als Kosmosophie* [Anthroposophy as cosmosophy] (GA 208), lectures of 12 and 13 November 1921.

11. *Das esoterische Christentum und die geistige Führung der Menschheit* [Esoteric Christianity and the spiritual guidance of humanity] (GA 130), lecture of 9 January 1912.
12. *Das Sonnenmysterium und das Mysterium von Tod und Auferstehung* [The Sun Mystery and the Mystery of death and resurrection] (GA 211), lectures of 21 and 24 March 1922.
13. *Esoterische Betrachtungen karmischer Zusammenhänge* [Esoteric studies of karmic relationships] (GA 236), lecture of 18 May 1924.
14. *Die Schwelle der geistigen Welt* [The threshold of the spiritual world] (GA 17), 'On Repeated Earth Lives and Karma'.
15. *Wie kann die Menschheit den Christus wiederfinden? Das dreifache Schattendasein unserer Zeit und das neue Christus-Licht.* [How can humanity find the Christ again? The threefold shadow existence of our age and the new the Christ-light] (GA 187), lecture of 27 December 1918.
16. *Gemeinsamkeit über uns, Christus in uns* [Community above us, Christ in us] (GA 159/160), lecture of 15 June 1915; *Wie kann die seelische Not der Gegenwart überwunden werden?* [How can the poverty of soul in the present time be overcome?] (GA 168), lecture of 10 October 1916; *Was tut der Engel in unserem Astralleib* [The work of the angel in our astral body] (GA 182), lecture of 9 October 1918.
17. *Ursprung und Ziel des Menschen* [Origin and goal of the human being] (GA 53), lecture of 16 March 1905.
18. *Theosophie* [Theosophy] (GA 9), chapter on 'The Essential Nature of Man', part 4 ('Body, Soul and Spirit').
19. *Von Jesus zu Christus* [From Jesus to the Christ] (GA 131), lecture of 12 October 1911.
20. *Esoterische Betrachtungen karmischer Zusammenhänge* [Esoteric studies of karmic relationships] (GA 237, 238, and 240), lectures beginning 6 July 1924.
21. *Esoterische Betrachtungen karmischer Zusammenhänge* [Esoteric studies of karmic relationships] (GA 239), lecture of 11 June 1924.
22. Ibid. (GA 237), lecture of 6 July 1924.

Notes   47

23. Ibid. (GA 240), lecture of 18 July 1924.
24. Ibid. (GA 240), lecture of 14 August 1924.
25. Ibid. (GA 238), lecture of 16 September 1924.
26. Ibid. (GA 237), lecture of 8 August 1924.
27. Ibid. (GA 240), lecture of 14 August 1924.
28. Ibid. (GA 240), lecture of 27 August 1924.
29. Ibid. (GA 240), lecture of 21 August 1924.
30. Ibid. (GA 237), lecture of 8 August 1924.
31. *Die Impulsierung des weltgeschichtlichen Geschehens durch geistige Mächte* [The movement of world-historical events by spiritual powers] (GA 222), lectures of 16, 17, and 18 March 1923.
32. *Initiations-Erkenntnis* [Initiation knowledge] (GA 227), lecture of 31 August 1923.
33. *Die Polarität von Dauer und Entwicklung im Menschenleben* [The polarity of permanence and development in human life] (GA 184), lectures of 11, 12 and 13 October 1918; see also *Wie finde ich den Christus?* [How do I find the Christ?] (GA 182), lecture of 16 October 1918.
34. *Von Jesus zu Christus* [From Jesus to Christ] (GA 131), lecture of 14 October 1911.
35. *Geistige Hierachien und ihre Widerspiegelung in der physischen Welt* [Spiritual hierarchies and their reflection in the physical world] (GA 110), evening lecture of 18 April 1909.
36. *Die Evolution vom Gesichtspunkte des Wahrhaftigen* [Evolution from the standpoint of what is true] (GA 132), lecture of 5 December 1911.
37. *Geschichtliche Symptomatologie* [Historical symptomatology] (GA 185), lectures of 25 and 25 October 1918.
38. *Vorstufen zum Mysterium von Golgotha* [Preparations for the Mystery of Golgotha] (GA 152), lecture of 2 May 1913.
39. *Esoterische Betrachtungen karmischer Zusammenhänge* [Esoteric studies of karmic relationships] (GA 240), lectures of 19 and 20 July 1924.
40. *Mysterienstätten des Mittelalters* [Mystery places of the Middle Ages] (GA 233a), lecture of 13 January 1924.

41. *Esoterische Betrachtungen karmischer Zusammenhänge* [Esoteric studies of karmic relationships] (GA 237), lecture of 4 August 1924.
42. Ibid., lecture of 8 August 1924.
43. *Die Philosophie der Freiheit* [The philosophy of freedom] (GA 4), chapter 9, 'The Idea of Freedom.'
44. *Von Jesus zu Christus* [From Jesus to Christ] (GA 131), lectures of 7 and 14 October 1911.
45. *Das Schicksalsjahr 1923 in der Geschichte der Anthroposophischen Gesellschaft* [1923: Year of destiny in the history of the Anthroposophical Society] (GA 259), address of 2 September 1923.
46. *Esoterische Betrachtungen karmischer Zusammenhänge* [Esoteric studies of karmic relationships] (GA 238), lecture of 28 September 1924.
47. Ibid. (GA 240), lecture of 21 August 1924.
48. *Das Markus-Evangelium* [The Gospel of Mark] (GA 139), lectures of 17, 18, and 20 September 1912.
49. *Das esoterische Christentum und die geistige Führung der Menschheit* [Esoteric Christianity and the spiritual guidance of humanity] (GA 130), lecture of January 9, 1912.
50. *Die Weihnachtstagung zur Begründung der Allgemeinen Anthroposophischen Gesellschaft* 1923/24 [The Christmas conference for the founding of the General Anthroposophical Society 1923/24] (GA 260).

Bibliography of books by Rudolf Steiner

GA (*Gesamtausgabe* or Collected Works)

4	*The Philosophy of Freedom / The Philosophy of Spiritual Activity*
9	*Theosophy*
10	*Knowledge of the Higher Worlds / How to Know Higher Worlds*
17	*Road to Self Knowledge and The Threshold of the Spiritual World*
31	*Gesammelte Aufsätze zur Kultur- und Zeitgeschichte 1887–1901*
53	*Sprung und Ziel des Menschen*
110	*The Spiritual Hierarchies*
130	*Esoteric Christianity and the Mission of Christian Rosenkreutz*
131	*From Jesus to Christ*
132	*Inner Realities of Evolution*
139	*The Gospel of St. Mark*
152	*Approaching the Mystery of Golgotha*
159/60	*Wesen und Bedeutung Mitteleuropas und die europäischen Volksgeister*
168	*Die Verbindung zwischen Lebenden und Toten*
182	*Der Tod als Lebenswandlung*
185	*From Symptom to Reality in Modern History*
186	*Die soziale Grundforderung unserer Zeit – In geänderter Zeitlage*
187	*How Can Mankind Find the Christ?*
208	*Cosmosophy Vol. 2*
211	*The Sun Mystery and The Mystery of Death and Resurrection*
222	*The Driving Force of Spiritual Powers in World History*
227	*The Evolution of Consiousness*

50 The Anthroposophical Society as a Michael Community

233a   Rosicrucianism and Initiation
236   Karmic Relationships Vol. II
237   Karmic Relationships Vol. III
238   Karmic Relationships Vol. IV
239   Karmic Relationships Vol. V
240   Karmic Relationships Vol. VI + VIII
258   The Anthroposophic Movement
259   Das Schicksalsjahr 1923 in der Geschichte der Anthroposophischen Gesellschaft
260   The Christmas Conference
266/3   Aus den Inhalten der esoterischen Stunden. Gedächtnisaufzeichnungen von Teilnehmern. Band III: 1913 and 1914; 1920–1923

English titles available from Rudolf Steiner Press, UK: www.rudolfsteinerpress.com or SteinerBooks, USA: www.steinerbooks.org